ISBN 978-1-332-18933-5
PIBN 10295859

For support please visit www.forgottenbooks.com

English
Français
Deutsche
Italiano
Español
Português

www.forgottenbooks.com

Mythology Photography **Fiction**
Fishing Christianity **Art** Cooking
Essays Buddhism Freemasonry
Medicine **Biology** Music **Ancient
Egypt** Evolution Carpentry Physics
Dance Geology **Mathematics** Fitness
Shakespeare **Folklore** Yoga Marketing
Confidence Immortality Biographies
Poetry **Psychology** Witchcraft
Electronics Chemistry History **Law**
Accounting **Philosophy** Anthropology
Alchemy Drama Quantum Mechanics
Atheism Sexual Health **Ancient History**
Entrepreneurship Languages Sport
Paleontology Needlework Islam
Metaphysics Investment Archaeology
Parenting Statistics Criminology
Motivational

REPORT

ON THE

RECONSTRUCTION

OF

INDUSTRY

Prepared after a series of

CONFERENCES

OF

PLYMOUTH AND CORNISH CITIZENS

who were also Employers and Trade Unionists,

HELD AT

PLYMOUTH

IN

MARCH and APRIL, 1918.

ALSO

Rules of the Devon and Cornwall Association for Industrial and
Commercial Reconstruction.

Price 3d.

The Conferences, which were held at first in separate groups and subsequently in joint session, were attended by the following, who were present in an individual and not in any representative capacity:—

EMPLOYERS.

Mr. Wm. Bate.
Mr. J. P. Brown, J.P.
Mr. Lovell Dunstan.
Mr. A. N. Hollely.
Mr. R. Martin.
Mr. H. G. Murdoch.

Mr. L. E. Strong.
Mr. J. Vivian Thomas.
Mr. W. H. Watkins.
Mr. W. Webber.
Mr. John Charles Williams.

TRADE UNIONISTS.

Mr. D. Hillman.
Miss Holland.
Miss F. Honeywill.
Mr. Stanley Johns.
Mr. H. M. Medland.

Mr. J. J. H. Moses.
Mr. G. Neilson.
Mr. J. Smale, J.P.
Mr. Percy S. Urell.
Mr. F. H. West.

Messrs. C. F. Aubone Hare and E. H. C. Wethered, of Bristol, also assisted.

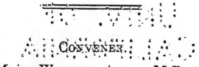

CONVENER.

Major Waldorf Astor, M.P.,

to whom all inquiries should be addressed at:—

3, Elliot-terrace,
Plymouth.

I.

GENERAL CONSIDERATIONS.

(1) The central feature of the industrial situation in Great Britain before the War was the want of confidence, mutual distrust, and suspicion between Capital and Management and Labour. This jealousy and lack of co-operation and of understanding also frequently separated employers and Trade Unions engaged in or connected with identical industries in the same areas.

(2) The War has created a sense of national unity against a common foe; has developed the idea of citizenship and disinterested service; and has forced a recognition of the fact that no section of the community is wholly bad or wholly good, but that each possesses to a large extent the same qualities and failings.

The situation has accordingly been materially altered. A real desire has been created among the leaders of both sides to unite in the work of reconstructing the country and world for which men of all classes are laying down their lives.

This spirit is strengthened by the growing recognition that human misery, discord, and poverty are common foes which all should join in trying to eliminate.

If this war-time vision of the future can be seized and translated into a normal outlook—if the country can in its everyday life approach more nearly to its professed ideals—if having united to overthrow irresponsible autocracy and jealous suspicion from the international world we can co-operate in a determined endeavour to remove the same causes of friction from our national industrial world, then great as have been our sacrifices and losses we believe that they will sink into relative insignificance compared with the incalculable benefit which must accrue to our people.

(3) The old distrust and suspicion which nevertheless continue to exist in wide circles on both sides may even be aggravated by special difficulties created by the war, and will become manifest again when the German danger at present threatening the country is removed, unless effective steps are taken, in time, to promote better relations. This risk is aggravated by the fact that the majority of the most prominent persons connected with industry have been so busy on war work that hitherto they have hardly found time to meet and

think out the best way of preventing a national catastrophe after the war.

(4) Until co-operation based on solid understanding is arrived at any substantial progress towards better relations is impossible.

It is, therefore, the manifest duty of every employer of and leader of labour to use his whole influence to build up a better order.

(5) No palliatives will suffice. The causes which have created and kept alive distrust and suspicion must be ascertained, faced, and removed.

II.

CAUSES OF DISTRUST AND SUSPICION.

The main causes of unrest and suspicion are:—

(a) The dissociation of the operatives from any share in the control of industry or responsibility for the conditions under which it is carried on.

(b) Mutual ignorance of each other's point of view between all sections engaged in or connected with industry.

(c) The suspicion of profiteering and the claim of the operatives to a greater share in the profits of industry.

(d) The fear of unemployment and the consequences which follow for the operatives.

(e) The reluctance of some employers to recognise the Trade Unions and to organise themselves in Federations.

Dealing in order with these causes:—

(a) THE QUESTION OF STATUS:—

The human problems involved in our commercial and industrial affairs must be taken into account in the work of reconstruction which lies ahead. In the past they have been too largely ignored.

The purely autocratically managed business is passing. The ideals for which the British Empire is fighting, namely, the overthrow of autocracy, must be applied to industry. In future the workers should be associated in the control of the industry in which they work and by which they live. Many industrial disputes in the past have been connected with questions of "management and discipline," and have not been due to differences over hours and wages. No single class, whether of employers or of employees, should monopolise the direction of business. The operatives are no longer content to occupy the position of mere servants, to receive and obey orders without question. They claim to be treated as fellow-workers and are desirous of sharing responsibility with Capital and Management (which is, in fact, only another form of employment). Labour has shown itself capable of finding men and women competent to undertake this. We believe that as Labour acquires greater power it will develop a greater sense of collective responsibility and be prepared to shoulder a greater measure of responsibility.

The primary demand of Labour to-day is not merely an economic, but is also a " human " demand. The operatives demand the recognition by employers and managers that they are intelligent human beings—men and women with the rights of citizenship in a Democratic State, and not merely servants or cogs in the wheels of the industrial machine. At present employers and employed are, too often, separated by something akin to a barrier of " caste," the most formidable of all barriers in social life. The operatives feel that they are frequently regarded by employers as beings of an inferior order and consequently they have come to regard their employers as members of another and of an antagonistic class.

This distrust often has been accentuated by the inability of employees—untrained in dialectics—to state their case in disputes, and of both sides to make the other understand their point of view. Such a failure has often left them sore and resentful.

We believe that there has existed a radically false conception of human life and society, which has produced an intense class bitterness.

Before any permanent improvement is possible these false views must be eradicated, and replaced by an entirely different outlook on life, based on a frank recognition of the solidarity of society.

If a new social order, based on fraternity, is to be built up, class consciousness must be avoided—just as class war and economic (civil) war must be avoided. The principles of co-operation and national service which the war have brought out must become the guiding principles in industry. All connected with industry must feel they are there to serve the State and not to get as much money as possible.

A new spirit is needed.

This new spirit must proceed from a new conception of commerce and industry, and of the consideration due to human life and personality. Commerce and industry must be considered in relation to the national life as a whole and be viewed as essential national services.

The creation and maintenance of physically sound and mentally developed men and women must be regarded as a definite object for which the community, as a whole, is responsible, and commerce and industry must be re-organised to serve this end. Industry is made for man and not man for industry.

If—but only if—this principle is frankly accepted and acted upon by Capital, Management, and Labour, we believe that the difficulties of industrial reconstruction can be overcome without a national catastrophe.

It is not too much to say that the future of civilisation depends on the spread of this new spirit, and the new sense of social responsibility which proceeds from it, in every sphere of human activity.

We welcome the growing recognition of this spirit. We feel it is hypocrisy to talk of a League of Nations or to expect anything from such a League so long as the peoples of this nation are not banded together for the orderly conduct of national affairs.

We desire to place on record, at the very forefront of this Report, the urgent need for the recognition and adoption of this new spirit by the Government where it is concerned with industry. The Government and municipal official is as much in need of a new outlook and conception of industry as the director in a private firm. Public ownership where it has failed has done so because of the absence of such a spirit and human touch. The principles of co-operation, responsibility, and self-government are as necessary in nationalised or municipalised as in privately owned businesses.

(*b*) MUTUAL IGNORANCE OF EACH OTHER'S POINT OF VIEW ON ·
  THE PART OF CAPITAL AND MANAGEMENT AND LABOUR :—

A lamentable ignorance exists among employers and employed as to the points of view, aspirations, needs, and difficulties of the other side as well as of each other.

It is not sufficient to wait for, or rely upon, better educational provision for the children. The adult population, employers, employed, and consumers, needs educating with regard to the social and economic considerations which apply to industry.

Informal meetings between individuals or groups of employers and employed should be held without delay all over the country for an intimate exchange of views on these problems.

The dangerous lack of understanding and sympathy between the individuals who compose the groups, into which those engaged in industry are at present divided, tends to be perpetuated because employers live too far apart from those they employ. Employers and employees rarely meet on a footing of frank and free equality. Such meetings as do occur are usually either of too formal or official a character, giving little scope for sympathetic understanding, or else occur too often as the result and at moments of acute industrial strife. Meetings between employers and employed, conceived as meetings between fellow-workers in a common cause, should be encouraged, and should be adopted as a permanent part of the conduct of industry.

(c) THE CLAIM OF THE OPERATIVES TO A GREATER SHARE IN THE PRODUCT OF INDUSTRY:—

An equitable division of the wealth created in industry among those responsible for its production is essential. It is conceded by all taking part in this Conference that in many cases the operatives, in the past, have not had the share to which they were fairly entitled. In others they have suspected the making of huge profits when this was not the case. The operatives have seen wealth created largely as the result of their efforts, and felt that they were entitled to a greater share in it. Frequently, too, they have seen the charges on industry enormously increased by the watering of capital—charges which have diminished the money available for distribution in wages while creating an additional return on capital which it had not earned. They also want wages to be fixed, not on a subsistence basis, but on the basis of a fair share in the product of the industry in which they are engaged. They desire an income which will enable their families to enjoy more fully the essentials and the amenities of life and also enable them to make reasonable provision for bad times.

(d) THE FEAR OF UNEMPLOYMENT:—

The fear of unemployment is in particular the cause of widespread bitterness and unrest. As things are at present, under a system of practically unrestrained competition, the operative is always in a position of insecurity as to his income, knowing that at short notice he is liable, at any time, to be paid off, whenever the exigencies of trade require a diminished output. At the same time he is usually excluded from any share in the control of the industry upon which his livelihood depends. Under such circumstances, it is idle to talk to him of the laws of supply and demand. He is faced with the human consequences of being without employment and with the practical difficulty of providing for his wife and family. Inevitably, having no responsibility himself, he blames the industrial system, with which he identifies his employer, and charges both it and him with inhumanity.

Thus distrust and unrest are steadily fed.

There has been widespread belief that a high rate of production leads to over-production, and that, when this happens, the demand for labour falls off, employees are discharged, and the operatives find themselves thrown out of work as the *result of their own efforts*. Whether economically sound or not, this belief has been one, if not the chief, of the causes tending to retard production.

The cutting of piece rates by certain employers, not because they were too high but because they enabled men to earn considerable sums, has also been a source of grievance and has hampered output.

The fear of causing unemployment and thereby taxing the funds of Trade Unions is another cause which has led to restriction of output.

Realising the foregoing points and the difficulties they raise we desire to state it as our opinion that to pay for the war and to maintain the necessary number of men and women in industry after the war we must increase production largely.

One of the best ways of securing the fullest possible production would be to secure the workers against the risk of unemployment, and to secure a large and safe market for the products of industry.

The profits of industry should in the future be prepared to bear more of the charges connected with unemployment, etc., which in the past have been borne either mainly or largely by the State or Trade Unions.

With reference to the deliberate restriction of output which has existed in some trades, we think it only right to express our opinion that frequently the more efficient workmen have deliberately elected to forego the earnings they could have secured for themselves, because they have felt that this policy was necessary in order to secure justice for their less skilful fellow workers. We hope it may be possible to obtain justice—where it is needed—by less uneconomic procedure.

(e) THE RELUCTANCE OF SOME EMPLOYERS TO RECOGNISE TRADE UNIONS AND TO ORGANISE THEMSELVES :—

The right of the operatives to seek to advance their standard of life by means of combination must be frankly recognised. The Trade Union movement has done much to create in the country the deeper sense of social responsibility already noticed. It has been a real educational and moral, as well as an economic, force.

The Unions are now an integral part of our industrial organisation, and are capable of rendering immense service to the proper conduct of industry. They are not only of advantage to the operatives, but should be so to the employers as well.

The policy of refusing recognition to the Unions is, in our opinion, mischievous and futile.

The principle of collective bargaining is sound, and should be widely extended. It should be the definite policy of employers not only to encourage and strengthen the Labour Organisations, but themselves to join and strengthen Employers' Federations, not for the purpose of antagonism but for consultation and co-operation.

The Government Departments and Municipalities ought to change their attitude towards collective bargaining and set an example to private enterprise. We welcome the recognition of this principle by the Government, and desire to emphasise the urgency of its early application.

III.

SUGGESTIONS FOR INDUSTRIAL RECONSTRUCTION.

THE WHITLEY REPORTS.

We accept the proposals contained in the Whitley Reports —in particular we welcome the principles underlying them. We believe that they are based on the same conception of self-government, coupled with decentralisation and continuous consultation which is the basis of the British Constitution; which is one of the underlying motives for closer union between the members of the British Commonwealth; and which constitutes the best chance of success for a League of Nations.

(a) ORGANISED INDUSTRIES.

We understand the main points in the First Whitley Report to be :—

(1) That there should be a Joint National Council for every important organised industry on which employers and employees should be equally represented (the method of such representation being left to each side to decide, the only requirement laid down by the Whitley Committee being that the former should belong to a Masters' Federation and the latter to a Trade Union). We believe that the development of such trade councils will facilitate negotiation, expedite agreement, bring a wide range of subjects within the discussion of employers and employed, and make industrial settlements more lasting.

(2) That the aforementioned Councils should appoint their own chairmen in such manner as they may think fit. We understand that in a Council recently set up when the Chairman is an operative the Vice-Chairman is a manufacturer, and vice-versa,

and that these officers are elected alternately from each side for one year.

(3) That there should be District Councils for each industry based on the same principle of joint representation as between employers and employees.

(4) That similarly there should be Works Committees.

(5) That all the above bodies should meet regularly and frequently.

As we conceive the development of the scheme, the Industrial Council might eventually fill the same rôle for industry as Parliament does for domestic government—i.e., that of laying down the governing principles on which the industry should be run. (We note, too, the suggestion that at some later stage the State might give the sanction of law to the agreements made by the National Councils.)

These principles having been established for the industry as a whole would then be adapted for the purpose of administration to local circumstances by the District Councils, and would be given effect to by the Works Committees, which would also deal with other matters of a more local and domestic character.

We understand that Works Committees recently appointed in other districts deal with the following among other questions: 1. Interpretation of official orders and regulations. 2. Interpretation of Trade Union rules to individual shops. 3. Holidays. 4. Decisions of foremen. 5. Time-keeping. 6. Adjustment of piece rates. 7. Stoppage of bonus. 8. Output and costs. 9. Overtime. 10. General discipline. 11. Canteens. 12. Shop conditions, lavatories, etc.

Works Committees, to be successful (and we believe they may be the pivot of the reorganisation under discussion), must, as far as possible, be linked up through the masters' and men's associations with the District and National Councils, for it is essential that these Committees should not in constitution or methods of working discourage trade organisations.

It is further important that Works Committees, unless authorised to do so, should not touch questions which are subjects of agreements between Trade Unions and Employers' Associations.

District Councils, as stated above, would probably include in their sphere the carrying out and application of the general principles laid down by the Central National Council, making such variations as might be needed to meet local circumstances. One District Council for a whole industry in an area will, for instance, be an improvement on the existing system of having several District Railway

Conciliation Boards which, working for separate companies, often act independently and on different lines in the same locality. We understand that the Plymouth Trades Council have already tried for other reasons to group local Trade Unions by industries.

(b) UNORGANISED INDUSTRIES.

The foregoing proposals apply to highly organised industries. Industries which are less well organised or which are practically unorganised are dealt with in the Second Whitley Report, which is still being considered by the Government.

These latter proposals, as we understand them, are as follows:—

That in all unorganised industries Trade Boards should be established, which should be empowered not only to fix minimum wages, but also to deal with hours and to initiate and conduct inquiries. As these Trade Boards improve conditions and the organisations of employers and employees in industries which have hitherto been unorganised, it is contemplated that the Ministry of Labour, acting with and on the advice of these Trade Boards, should set up National Councils with representatives of the Ministry to advise at the outset. Eventually it is hoped that every industry will be sufficiently well organised to have its own Industrial Council on the lines laid down in the First Whitley Report.

STATE CONTROL.

We approve of the Whitley Committee's statement that the extent of State assistance should vary inversely with the degree of organisation in industries.

We have not attempted, in our Conferences or in this Report, to define or analyse the full and potential scope of the Whitley proposals. This would not be either possible or wise. Sufficient is it to say that the scheme lays down sound fundamental principles on which can be built a structure for industrial government as experience is acquired. We welcome the fact that no limit or restriction is placed on this growth by the Whitley Committee.

Lastly, we observe with satisfaction that the Industrial Councils will be recognised as the official Standing Consultative Committees to the Government on all future questions affecting the industries which they represent, and that they will be the normal channel through which the opinion and experience of an industry will be sought.

PUBLICITY.

We desire to urge that where necessary monthly journals should be published containing a summary of the proceedings and decisions of National and District Councils and of Works Committees. Publicity is the life-blood of the movement.

We have been struck, not only by the lack of knowledge as to what was being done in different parts of the country, but also by the widespread desire on the part of many associated with industry to understand the proposals and to take an intelligent and substantial share in industrial reconstruction.

PROFITS.

We have had to refer on several occasions to profits. In our opinion capital is entitled to a fair interest for its employment, in the same way as labour is paid a wage for the use and employment of its physical and mental capacity and skill, which represent its capital. In both cases the financial return must vary according to risks run and other factors. But after admitting the foregoing principle, we desire to record our view that either within certain limitations the profit on capital should be restricted or that any surplus or excess profit made should not go entirely to the capital employed in industry.

This surplus profit can be given either as a whole or in varied proportions to:—

(1) The State (by taxation, e.g., income tax and excess profits tax).

(2) The industry as a whole, e.g., profit sharing, payment to reserves, etc.

(3) A single element in industry, e.g., to Capital by increased profits or to Labour by higher wages, unemployment fund, etc.

(4) The consumers (e.g., the discount of Co-operative Societies).

When examining the above possible uses of surplus profit, certain considerations presented themselves to us:—

(a) If the surplus is due to a monopoly then it should, generally speaking, go to the community.

(b) If the surplus is due to exceptional efficiency within the industry, then the firm or firms showing such special efficiency within the industry have a special claim to it.

(c) The present unrestricted individual or collective right of bargaining and competition is apt to cause the wholesale and retail price of goods to be determined on a false basis, i.e., a basis not necessarily related to the cost of production, even after making allowance for the cost of distribution, etc.

(d) One way of regulating profits would be by fixing the retail price of an article on its cost of production after allowing a fair wage, a fair salary, a fair rate of interest, and a reasonable margin for certain necessary trade contingencies and a fair charge for the cost of distribution.

In our judgment this would be fair to all the elements in industry, and would give the consumer greater protection than he now possesses.

But we realise that before such a basis could be at all generally applied, a far more scientific system of management and of ascertaining costs would have to be adopted than is now immediately feasible on a big scale.

It is also necessary not to lose sight of the fact that unless Capital (which bears the risks) gets some part —even if only a smaller part than hitherto—of the surplus profit, it may lack the necessary stimulus and incentive and may tend to play too much for safety.

(e) The retail price of an article should not be determined by the inefficient firms, as this enables efficient firms to make excessive profits at the expense of the community, and the inefficient firms to sweat their employees.

(f) The mobility of capital must not be forgotten. Unequal or penal treatment of capital as compared with its treatment in other countries might have most serious consequences for industry.

We believe that there is an increasing feeling among holders of capital that they should use it to a greater extent than hitherto to the national advantage or for the more general benefit of mankind.

(g) If the profits of capital are to be restricted and capital is to receive a smaller reward for the considerable risks it must occasionally take, and if Labour is to be given not only greater security and a higher minimum wage, but also some share in surplus profits, whether this be by profit-sharing, higher wages, the creation of a reserve for unemployment, or by other means, then there is bound to be a demand that Labour should in some way bear some of the risks and losses connected with the conduct of industry.

(h) The present inequality of earnings (whether these be represented by wages or profits on capital or salaries) between persons engaged in or connected with different industries raises important issues. Certain industries are able now and do for various reasons give to those engaged in those industries incomes far in excess of the incomes earned by equally competent individuals in other industries in the same area.

It does not seem fair that men in a certain industry, because it has been badly organised in the past or because of any other special reasons, should receive a much smaller income than men in another industry, even though both may be doing equal work, making an equal effort, and relatively showing equal aptitude.

The broad conclusions we have arrived at are that (1) there must be a more equitable and inclusive distribution of surplus profit; that is to say, the profit which remains after the payment (i.) to capital of interest (which must not only be fair, but also adequate to attract capital) and (ii.) proper trade charges (e.g., depreciation, payment to reserve, etc.) have been met; and (2) that as one of the results of the better organisation of industry the *minimum* returns to capital, labour and management respectively is likely to be more equalised as between different industries in the country.

War has made people realise more fully that there are higher motives than material gain and self protection. We believe it is becoming increasingly appreciated that every man is, in fact, his brother's keeper, and that the mere struggle for bare life must be replaced by a seeking after a better life.

In our opinion much of the friction and disturbance connected with industry in the past has been due to either (1) the employers or shareholders making excessive profits, or (2) the men suspecting the existence of excessive profits, when this was not actually the case, or (3) inefficient organisation and absence of up-to-date business methods which impeded the paying of fair wages and the making of reasonable profits. We believe that under the proposed reorganisation and co-operation it will be possible for the Whitley Industrial Councils to give to all firms in an industry the *average* costs of production and other essential facts for the whole of the industry (without, of course, disclosing particulars connected with any individual firm). Such informaton should be of incalculable advantage to firms engaged in the industry. Further, this greater information on the financial factors of industry either will enable the workers to claim that proper share in the prosperity of their industry to which we believe they are entitled or will allay any unfounded suspicion that may have existed as to profiteering. We understand that already the National Potteries Council have proposed to disclose to the employees' representatives on the Council the figures as to costs of production, etc. This is a big step forward, and one well calculated to allay suspicion and improve relations.

We believe that it may also be advisable and necessary to publish these figures of average costs of production after they have been duly audited. Unless this is done an industry might unreasonably raise its payments to the interests engaged in or connected with it to the serious prejudice and detriment of the general body of consumers.

The State should be prepared to interfere and protect the interests of consumers and prevent their being exploited by a monopoly or anything approaching thereto should such exploitation be threatened.

FOREMEN.

The selection and training of foremen and forewomen is an important matter, owing to the part they play in the relations between employers and employed. Their position is often difficult. The foreman has duties, not only to his employers, but to the people over whom he is put in authority. Often greater care should be taken to select the right type of man or woman for this office, and steps should be taken with the object of educating foremen and forewomen, so that they may be better fitted to discharge their duties. They need training and instruction, not only in the technical details and the policy of their trade, but in the handling of men and women.

We put forward the following alternative tentative proposals for meeting an admittedly difficult problem:—

    (1) That in large firms the employer should appoint a small panel from which the employees should select the actual foreman.

    (2) That a foreman should not be appointed or continued in office in face of reasoned opposition.

DISCHARGE.

We realise that so long as the employer alone is financially responsible for the industry (including the payment of wages) he must have the final decision as to the date of termination of engagement with his employees. But we feel bound to record the fact that the uncontrolled right of dismissal and its arbitrary use is and has been a deep cause of ill-feeling on the part of employees conscious of the human consequences to their families which are apt to follow.

We believe that a distinction can be drawn between (1) summary dismissal for misconduct or other reason and (2) discharge on the ending of a contract. If the ending of an engagement be approached more as a dissolution of partnership and less as the dismissal of a servant it should be possible to protect not only the economic rights of the employer, but also the moral rights of the employee by some right of appeal to an impartial tribunal.

If possible a foreman should not have the power of dismissal without reference or appeal either to the Management or to a Works Committee and without giving any reason for such dismissal.

IV.

INDUSTRIAL PEACE.

(a) ARBITRATION AND CONCILIATION.

At present statutory compulsory arbitration would be strenuously resisted by Organised Labour, and we do not believe that we are yet ready to settle all disputes without reservation by peaceful methods. But in our opinion both sides should agree voluntarily to go to arbitration, if, *and after*, conciliation fails. If such a course be voluntarily agreed to, we feel that in most cases arbitration should not be undertaken by a single arbitrator, but by an Arbitration Court on the model of the Munition Tribunals, consisting of a chairman with a legal training and two or more technical assessors, representing and chosen from panels of employers and employed respectively.

We also favour statutory *compulsory conciliation* with the object of effecting a settlement of differences and avoiding resort to a strike or lock-out.

This is, in our view, consistent with the proposed League of Nations. In fact, any other course would be inconsistent with such a proposal. If we are engaged in waging a war to end war, if we desire to have negotiation and arbitration between nations on the most vital international questions, then we believe that those connected with industry will have to be prepared to adopt the same mode of settling internal disputes over relatively minor issues. In our opinion the tendency against the arbitrament of war, i.e., the appeal to force, will have to be applied to the world of industry, that is to say, that at some future time arbitration will have to replace the strike and lock-out.

In industrial disputes the Government should be empowered and encouraged to bring the parties together without having to wait for an invitation. The Conciliation Board should have an independent chairman, and should have powers to call for documents, witnesses, etc.

In the event of an agreement not being arrived at, the chairman should be required to make a report on the difference, with his opinion thereon; this report should appear in the Press, and should be published verbatim. We believe that public opinion would compel agreement on a reasonable basis after the facts had been published and understood. We realise that negotiation has in some quarters become unpopular because it has enabled recalcitrants to delay decisions. This, we think, depends on machinery and procedure. We are agreed that distrust is apt to arise from protracted negotiations, and that the *essence of successful conciliation is rapid action*. We are also agreed that long-term agreements are dangerous.

(*b*) INDUSTRIAL COURTS.

In view of the large amount, and the probable extension, of industrial legislation, we are of opinion that a new type of Court is needed, consisting of a Chairman with legal training, who has specialised in industrial questions, with technical assessors, to take over from the County Court cases of the type of Workmen's Compensation claims, and from the Stipendiaries and Justices, cases such as proceedings under the Factory Acts and disputes under the Employers' and Workmen's Act. The costs incurred in these matters in the ordinary Courts are much too heavy, and the experience of the Munitions Tribunals seems to show that this expenditure is unnecessary.

V.

DEMOBILISATION AND ITS PROBLEMS.

The questions which will arise on Demobilisation are too numerous and complex to be dealt with fully or finally in such a report as this. We desire, however, to put forward certain views on specific points.

(*a*) EMPLOYMENT EXCHANGES.

The Employment Exchanges provide machinery which can be of considerable assistance in carrying out the work of demobilisation, but they need alteration.

We are of opinion that the system should be efficient enough to attract workers and employers, so that compulsory registration, in itself objectionable, need never become necessary. This involves the State, employers, and operatives co-operating in the management.

We believe that improvement might be made along the following lines:—

(1) That the Advisory Committees to the Exchanges should be given executive powers.

(2) That all labour should be encouraged to go through the Exchanges, and that the Exchanges should be prepared to register men, whether they are actually out of work or not.

(3) That the Managers of Exchanges should be men with lifelong experience of labour and industry.

(4) That there should be established a Central Clearing House in London directly connected with every local exchange by telephone and that information as to local demands for and supplies of labour should be ascertainable as between any two areas at any time of day without undue formality, and with power to authorise and pay for the transfer of labour from area to area.

Further, we think that new premises of a more ample and dignified character, in central sites, should be substituted for the present Employment Exchange buildings. Such a change will be necessary in view of the importance of the functions which, in our view, should be assigned to the Exchanges.

(b) THE RESTORATION OF TRADE UNION CUSTOMS, ETC.

We agree with the Whitley Committee that while all the lessons learnt during the war should not be ignored, none of the guarantees and undertakings given by the Government or by Parliament and by individual firms should be set aside without the acquiescence of the Trade Unions. If they are modified, they must be modified as the outcome of joint arrangement between employers and employed.

The following points arose during our conferences and bear on this question:—

(1) The entire upheaval of industry and the length of the war have made the complete fulfilment of the pledges impossible without there being any desire to break faith on the part of the Government or individual firms, who we believe will attempt to honour the bond if required to do so.

(2) Pre-war conditions were not satisfactory. Instead of insisting upon a blind return to them it is better to concentrate upon an advance and improvement.

(3) It is impossible to contemplate or advocate the immediate dismissal from their present jobs of all women who have taken the place of men in industry owing to the war.

(4) The loss due to war can only be repaired by a collective and national increase in production.

(c) WAGES.

In view of the fact that the fixing of wages will be one of the first duties and functions of the new industrial machinery and that we have not been able to give sufficient consideration to the question, we only desire to emphasise the importance of dealing with wages in a national spirit. We agree with the analysis of wages into (i.) a basic or minimum wage and (ii.) a secondary wage or supplementary income which an employee may earn as the result of acquired aptitude, extra effort, or natural physical or mental endowment. We are not prepared at this stage to lay down detailed conclusions on the principles which should be adopted for determining what the basic wage should be. We note the proposition that it should be fixed at such a sum as would enable a married man with two or three children to bring up his family decently. Against this the arguments are advanced that, although by this proposal a burden would be placed on industry which would be unnecessary, in that many male employees do not have to support a wife and two or three entirely dependent children, yet at the same time men with large families of five, six, or more dependents would not be enabled to maintain the intended standard of domestic life. It has also been suggested, and there is much to be said for the proposal, that the basis should be such a wage as would enable a man and wife to live decently, and that the man with dependents who is employed in industry should be helped by the State rather than by the industry—i.e., that more services should be rendered directly by the State in order to maintain a proper minimum standard of life for its citizens: e.g., more medical and maternity help, school feeding, free education up to and including the Universities might be provided. Some of us are inclined to suggest this alternative as giving relief to industry in view of the suggestion made under the section dealing with unemployment where we propose that industry should shoulder more of the burdens hitherto borne largely by the State or Trade Unions.

As regards the principle on which wages for women should be determined we are of opinion that women should get equal pay with men for equal work where the results accomplished are the same. In employments which are reserved for women only the minimum wage should enable a single woman to live respectably in a proper house after making all allowances for meeting reasonable contingencies.

Lastly we desire to say that we recognise the need of considering both local costs of living and also the present relative ability of various industries to increase their wage bill.

(d) HOURS.

We welcome the publication of the reports made for the Government by the Health of Munition Workers' Committee, and hope that their recommendations for shorter hours, weekly days of rest, etc., may be acted upon as far as possible.

(e) WOMEN.

We believe women share the growing desire of men for a fuller life and for a share both in shaping the future of the country and in serving it. The war, which has imposed such a burden of sorrow and anxiety on them, has proved the intensity of this sentiment, which we believe will be perpetuated by the recent extension of the franchise to the female sex.

The problems raised by the influx of women into industry are so diverse and complex that we do not as yet feel qualified to state more than a few somewhat general—but at the same time fundamental propositions.

We believe a large number of women will tend to be self-supporting in the future, either because they have lost their husbands or because war work has opened to them a new conception of life.

Many will not want to return to lives of semi-idleness, or to domestic service, unless more freedom is permitted in this latter. The death of so many males must further have diminished the chances of marriage for a large number of women who would normally have looked to matrimony as the most natural fulfilment of their life's purpose.

The outstanding fact remains that many women have been and are still receiving less than a living wage, whatever standard be adopted.

The pin-money girl, who is able to use her earnings wholly or mainly as pocket-money, bears a heavy burden of responsibility if she encourages the payment of a wage on which a less well-circumstanced girl cannot live in decency. This responsibility applies also to consumers.

Purchasers of goods which have been made by female sweated labour, leading to physical inefficiency, immorality, and overwork, which are the natural consequences of badly paid labour, cannot escape a share in responsibility. They fail in their duty as citizens and mothers and members of a Christian community if they condone and permit such a system merely because it is not constantly and inconveniently thrust before them.

Women will and must take many places in industry hitherto occupied by men, for many of them are not only skilled operatives, but have proved themselves competent managers. In our opinion the increased and continued employment of women must tend to augment production and so to increase the demand for labour generally.

As soon as an armistice is signed tens of thousands of women will be thrown out of employment and will present a problem of sufficient dimensions to cause us anxiety unless immediate steps are taken to prepare for it. The problem will be enormously magnified when the men as a whole are returned to industry from the army.

We welcome the proposal of many unions to admit women into their association, and we believe that the problems of demobilisation affecting women should be considered without loss of time by delegates from all the (Whitley) Industrial Councils meeting as a body, with representatives of organisations catering for female members.

After the War there will be a demand for male labour from the Dominions and Colonies, in order to repair the wastage of war, and to reinforce the overseas industries.

This will inevitably lead to a corresponding movement of women to the Dominions. Careful organisation will be necessary, both here and in the Dominions, to provide for proper care being taken of those who emigrate.

To ease the problem of reinstatement, the following classes might be excluded from industry on general social grounds when peace comes:—

> (a) Women with dependents (children or incapacitated husbands), who should receive adequate pensions. This provision should not be confined to women whose need is due to the War.

> (b) Children under (and, as far as possible, children of) school age. The entry of children into industry at too early an age is productive of great harm to the national life.

The two aspects of women's work, the economic aspect and the social aspect, should be clearly distinguished. The effect of different employments on the health and physique of women should be borne in mind. As a preliminary to, and as a part of the work of, demobilisation a commission might be set up at once to inquire into this problem. Investigation is showing that some classes of work performed by women are injurious to their health. To permit women to engage in such occupations is to endanger the highest interests of the State. The nucleus of such a commission is to be found in the Health of Munition Workers' Committee of the Ministry of Munitions, and the Home Office Factory Inspectors. Such a commission subsequently might be merged into the Ministry of Public Health if such a Ministry is established, as we believe it ought to be.

(f) OLD MEN.

We understand that in at least one large and highly organised industry superannuation is to begin five years earlier than heretofore. An extension of this principle would help to relieve the Labour market after the war.

(g) DISABLED SOLDIERS.

The position of disabled soldiers presents a series of problems particularly difficult of solution because we have but little experience to guide us. We are of opinion that:—

> (1) The training and re-education of disabled soldiers for civilian life should start as soon as their condition allows it, and as soon as they are passed unfit for further military service. The Army, which in this case represents the State, has on it the duty of restoring these men to civil life, not only with a pensions, but if possible fitted to add to and augment this pension by their own efforts.

(2) Disabled soldiers should be protected against any attempt to use them as cheap labour. Their pensions should not be allowed to count in the fixing of wages. It is necessary to assess (through some tribunal) the relation of a disabled man's earning capacity to the earning capacity of an able-bodied adult. As disabled men are getting on the labour market to an increasing extent, we look on this matter as one of urgency.

(3) It may be necessary to allocate specific industries for these men, as has been done with basket-making for the blind.

(*h*) BROKEN INDENTURES.

As regards " broken indenture," full rates should be paid for half the normal pre-war period. We base this on the understanding that men discharged from the Army owing to their being more mature and rendered quicker by their military training, are able to pick up a trade very much faster than young undeveloped and untrained men. It may be necessary, however, also to have supplementary indentures at special rates, with State financial assistance.

(*i*) SOLDIERS IN REMOTE DISTRICTS.

Discharged men whose homes are in remote and sparsely populated districts may experience difficulty in hearing of suitable work and in making their requirements known. County Pensions Committees might be put in touch with the Exchanges, and might increase the number and activities of their own sub-committees or agents. Where no other machinery is in existence, these Committees appear to us to be specially suited for the task, as they are already engaged in trying to place a certain number of discharged men (the disabled) in civil employment.

VI.

UNEMPLOYMENT.

We believe industry will have to shoulder more of the charges and burdens now borne mainly by the State and Trade Unions, and that industries as industries should pay unemployment benefit to the men connected with those industries for a period. Beyond this period the State would have to assume responsibility. Incidentally this might have the advantage of reducing cut-throat competition between firms. While unemployment benefit cannot be without limit and can only hope to provide maintenance for periods of normal trade fluctuations, or for the period of change from one firm to another on the part of individuals, we still feel that such benefit should approximate as far as possible to the normal earnings when at work and not be a mere pittance.

We appreciate the fact that the problem of unemployment in this country may be aggravated either immediately after the war or else at a latter date by dumping in the home market or underselling in outside markets. At some future time this threat may be eliminated (*a*) by international industrial agreement, as is being attempted in this nation between firms, or (*b*) by the fixing of wages internationally. Even were this latter possible now, the widely divergent national standards of life, not only between white peoples, but still more so between white and coloured, are material factors which would not be dealt with by such a remedy.

The fixing of minimum retail prices, if it were feasible, would help to meet the difficulty, but this is a policy not easy to enforce effectively without control of production from start to finish.

While desiring the minimum amount of Government interference or regulation, we appreciate the fact that owing to the shortage of tonnage, raw material, and foodstuffs, some form of international as well as of national control of distribution or allocation of these essentials is imperative at least for a time after the war.

Owing to the abnormal conditions created by the war we believe it may be necessarily temporarily to regulate home production ; to arrange for reserves of national or seminational work, and to spread industrial production in a regulated manner instead of allowing complete and free play to individual competitive output. If this is done it must be accompanied by some control of importation.

Perhaps the best method for obtaining some such control of domestic production as is referred to would be by the establishment of a Ministry of Supply. The demands of certain Government Departments, like the Office of Works, of our Dominions and Crown Colonies abroad, of our great municipalities at home are enormous in their totality. They represent a vast amount of goods and services which are not all needed with the same degree of urgency. A Ministry of Supply, properly informed by the Ministry of Labour as to the probable fluctuations of ordinary trade, could let loose in time of depression and withhold in time of prosperity demands for Government and municipal work. By such means trade would be steadied, bad trade being rendered less bad, and good trade less good. There would be less insecurity of employment for all.

RULES

OF

INDUSTRIAL AND COMMERCIAL RECONSTRUCTION ASSOCIATION.

In view of the fact that substantial agreement had been shown during the final discussions on many matters affecting the future industrial and commercial welfare of the country, and in view of the fact that many matters connected therewith still required careful investigation and discussion, those present at the end of the joint conference held on April 28, 1918, unanimously passed the following resolution:—

> That it is desirable to continue and enlarge the conferences under the auspices of a permanent association for the study of industrial and commercial reconstruction.

The following Rules and Regulations were also agreed to and passed:—

1.—The Association shall be called " The Devon and Cornwall Association for Industrial and Commercial Reconstruction."

2.—The objects of the Association shall be as follows:—

(i.) To further generally the task of Industrial and Commercial Reconstruction and Education.

(ii.) To give effect to the general policy, and principles contained in the Report of the Conferences held at Plymouth in March and April. 1918.

(iii.) To investigate industrial and commercial questions and social problems connected with industry and commerce, both in their general and local aspects.

(iv.) To help in forming similar bodies in Devon and Cornwall and, after the formation of such associations, to give and obtain information on matters of common interest.

3.—Any resident in Devonshire or Cornwall who is interested in or associated with industry and commerce and who is willing to give general assent to the objects of the Association may be admitted as a member of the Association if his or her name is put before the Executive Committee by two Employers and two Trade Unionists, and if he or she obtains the support of three-quarters of the Committee.

4.—An Ordinary Meeting of the Association shall, if possible, be held on the first Saturday in each month, at such time and place as may be determined by the Executive Committee.

5.—The officers of the Association shall be as follows, namely, a President, Vice-Presidents, a Treasurer, and a Secretary.

6.—The first officers shall continue in office until the first Annual General Meeting of the Association, unless previously removed at a Special Meeting of the Association called for that purpose. At the first and each succeeding Annual General Meeting of the Association the Association shall elect officers for the ensuing year. Such officers shall hold office until the next Annual General Meeting, unless previously removed at a Special Meeting called for that purpose. Retiring officers shall be eligible for re-election, and shall hold office until their successors are appointed.

7.—The business of the Association shall be conducted by an Executive Committee, which shall have control of all business carried on by or on account of the Association, subject nevertheless to such regulations or instructions as may from time to time be prescribed or given by a resolution of the Association at a General Meeting; provided that such regulations or instructions shall not invalidate any act of the Executive Committee prior to the passing of such resolution or giving of such instructions.

8.—The Executive Committee shall as far as possible consist of representatives of Employers and Trade Unionists in equal numbers, and shall be made up of the officers, together with not less than six unofficial members of the Association.

9.—The first unofficial members shall continue in office until the first Annual General Meeting of the Association, unless previously removed at a Special Meeting of the Association called for that purpose. At the first, and each succeeding, Annual General Meeting, one-third of the unofficial members shall retire from office, and the Association shall elect such number of unofficial members of the Association, not being less than two, as the Association may determine, to serve upon the Executive Committee. Retiring unofficial members shall be eligible for re-election, and shall hold office until their successors are appointed. The unofficial members to retire in each year shall be those who have been longest in office since their last election. As between members of equal seniority in office the members to retire (in default of agreement) shall be selected from amongst them by lot.

10.—If an officer or an unofficial member of the Executive Committee dies, or resigns, in the interval between two Annual General Meetings, the Association shall appoint a person to fill the vacancy until the next Annual General Meeting.

11.—An Annual General Meeting of the Association shall be held if possible in the month of May in each year, at such time and place as shall from time to time be determined by the Executive Committee.

12.—A Special General Meeting may be called at any time by the Executive Committee, and shall be called upon a requisition in writing of any six members. Such requisition shall be sent to the Secretary and shall state the purpose for which the meeting is to be called.

13.—Seven days' notice at least of every General and Ordinary Meeting, specifying the day, place and hour of the Meeting, and, in the case of special business, the general nature of such business, shall be sent to the members entitled to be present, but an accidental omission to send such notice to any member shall not invalidate the proceedings at any meeting.

14.—Each member of the Association shall pay a minimum half-yearly subscription of 2s. 6d.

15.—New Rules may be made, and existing Rules amended, varied or rescinded, with the assent of two-thirds of the number present and voting at a General Meeting of the Association specially called for the purpose.

16.—All members of affiliated Associations shall be honorary members.

17.—The Executive may invite persons who are not members to attend and take part in discussions on special occasions.

The following were appointed to be the first officers of the Association :—

President—Major Waldorf Astor.

Vice-Presidents—Mr. J. P. Brown, Mr. Stanley Johns, *Mr. P. S. Urell, Mr. John Charles Williams.

Treasurer—Mr. A. N. Hollely.

Secretary—Mr. W. Webber.

The following were appointed to be the first unofficial members of the Executive: Miss Honeywell and Messrs. Lovell Dunstan, H. G. Murdoch, G. Neilson, J. Smale, J. Vivian Thomas, and F. H. West.

* Mr. Urell was unable to accept the invitation to become a Vice-President.

CPSIA information can be obtained
at www.ICGtesting.com
Printed in the USA
BVHW071305311218
536776BV00015B/2790/P